WHAT REAL PEOPLE SAY ABOUT
A COMPANY OF ONE

"Thanks for proving independence is NOT a dirty word. The saddest employee I have is truly dependent on our company. *A Company of One* is a must for all such employees."
    Raymond Becker
    President
    Conductive Containers Inc.

"The move to high performance organizations will require individuals to be independent enough to have the confidence to do more risk taking, but interdependent enough to improve teamwork and communication. This material is a corner piece as corporate America begins to assemble the puzzle."
    Barbara Plante
    Organization Development Specialist
    INTEL Corporation

"The gist of *A Company of One* is right on target with what is needed in business today. I especially like the pragmatic "how to's" and the easy-to-understand approach to a very complicated issue."
    Mike Frazier
    Senior Manager
    Illinois Bell

"*A Company of One* gives us an insight into the framework needed to get this country moving again. Payne pinpoints how the independent, creative, self-confident employee can work productively for the mutual benefit of the individual and the organization. Great stuff."
    Frank Feist
    Vice President
    Coca Cola-United

"My company and my customers have both taken new directions for the 90's. I knew I had to carve a new path for myself. *A Company of One* helped me turn my path into a superhighway!"
    Craig Campbell
    Industry Sales Representative
    Snap-On Tools

"*A Company of One* addresses how some companies have depressed the independence of the worker.... Tom's book shows simple and precise methods of emerging from dependency. A must for a quality worker."
    John Sullivan
    Technician
    AMP Inc.

"Companies who fear *A Company of One* are losing the creative, confident employees that they will require for long term success."

>Gail Link
>National Sales Manager
>Federal Sign

"Lack of commitment may be the number one problem in business today. *A Company of One* provides the vision of how we can take care of ourselves by being committed to what is important."

>Rick Mack
>Program Manager
>City Of Albuquerque

"Tom Payne has done an outstanding job of identifying the tremendous need for each individual to take ownership for his or her career and to contribute their unique skills to the enhancement of the organization."

>Dennis Gorsuch
>Managing Director
>Right Associates

"In *A Company of One*, Tom Payne teaches us about control and the power we all possess to maximize our potentials. Organizations of the 90's must learn to empower their employees. Independent people who are committed to excellence will be more productive and successful professionally and personally."

>Christie Ahrens
>Classroom Teacher - School District 54, Illinois
>Instructor - National College of Education

"*A Company of One* is about what really makes the system work, the people, and their individual commitment to personal and organizational success. A must read!"

>Roy Moody
>President
>Roy Moody and Associates

"*A Company of One* is clear on what it takes for individuals to succeed and be happy within their organizations and how this spills over to their personal lives."

>Barney Fleming
>Marketing Director
>AT&T

"*A Company of One* does more than point out the power of independence in the workplace; it demonstrates the necessity."

>George Hartmann
>Corporate Vice President
>Fort Howard Corporation

A Company of One
The Power of Independence in the Workplace

Tom Payne

of Albuquerque.

A Company of One:

The Power of Independence in the Workplace

COPYRIGHT © 1993 by Thomas E. Payne

All rights reserved.

Written permission to reproduce portions of this book may be obtained from LODESTAR, 1200 Lawrence Court NE, Albuquerque, New Mexico 87123-1905.

Publisher's Cataloging in Publication Data

Payne, Thomas E.
A Company of One: The Power of Independence in the Workplace

1. Organizational effectiveness. 2. Success in business. 3. Self management.

HD58.9.P64   1993   658.4   92-91095
ISBN 0-9627085-4-2 $12.95 Soft Cover

COVER DESIGN & GRAPHICS: Dave Payne — Hodge Podge Lodge

First Printing 1993
Second Printing 1994

Printed in the United States of America

"Is the objective of your organization to keep you employed? If the answer is *no*, then whose objective is it to keep you employed?

How many people do you know who have a written employment contract with their employers? Short of that, we must take care of ourselves. It is not a matter of loyalty. It is a matter of business; each of us must become *a company of one*."

Excerpt from a speech by Tom Payne

A COMPANY OF ONE

is dedicated to and written for

PEOPLE

People who:

— are employed by someone else regardless of where their names appear on the organization chart.

OR

— wish to be employed by someone else.

With special acknowlegement to:

John Collins, Mike Frazier, Milt Garrett Ed.D., Joelle Hertel, Barbara Jones, Steven Keene, Rick Nelson, Pauline Taylor and to the person without whom I would be an only child, Bill Payne. Thanks for all your work on my behalf.

Also a special thanks to my sons, Dave and Tom, who have added a unique perspective, each in his own way, to both this book and my life.

Finally I wish to recognize the significant contributions of my editor, researcher, advisor and life partner, Jean. Without you none of this would have happened.

Tom Payne

Table of Contents

SECTION ONE
INDEPENDENCE

1. A Company of One —
   What Does That Mean?   10
2. Independence -
   What It Is and What It Isn't   13
3. It Is Time for Independence   15
4. The Independence Paradox   19
   "Most of Our People Do Not"   19
   How Did We Get Dependent?   22
   The Independence Paradox   24
   Isn't Independence Tough on Organizations?   26
   Shouldn't We Strive for Interdependence?   27
   Recap   29

SECTION TWO
ORGANIZATION

5. Organizational Benefits of Independence   32
   The Mobile Work Force   32
   Maslow Revisited   35
   Doing Less with More   39
   Teams of Individuals   41
   Silent Majority   43
   A New Loyalty   45
   Compensate Our Way to Productivity   48
   Recap   50
6. Organizational Downsides of a Culture
   of Independence   52
7. How to Create an Organizational Culture
   of Independence   55

SECTION THREE
PERSONAL

8. Personal Benefits of Independence	60
The Monkeys in the Jar	60
The Control/Stress Relationship	62
Why Choose Independence	65
Who Is Going to Do All the Work?	68
R-E-S-P-E-C-T	70
Retraining the Organization	72
A Country Drug Store	75
A Big Mistake	78
Recap	80
9. Personal Downsides of Independence	82
10. How to Create a Personal Culture of Independence	86

SECTION FOUR
ACTION

11. Personal Business Plan	93
12. New Employment Contract	96

SECTION FIVE
WRAP UP

13. Independence — How It Sounds on the Job	102
14. Traits of an Independent Person	107
15. What Others Have to Say	109
16. Some Last Words	113
17. A Declaration of Independence	115

INDEPENDENCE
What's it all about?

SECTION ONE

A COMPANY OF ONE — WHAT DOES THAT MEAN?

A *company of one* is a person who views and conducts himself or herself as a business entity. This business, due to experience, education and passion, possesses unique skills and regards those skills as a high quality inventory of services which are available for sale or barter.

Those words may sound like they were written by a committee of five on staff of a major corporation. Let me explain a *company of one* the way I think of it.

The *company of one* is the independent you. Your *company of one* has a varied and unique inventory.

Your inventory is the hard earned skills you have developed through all of your life. Some of your skills are common and some unique. You have in the past parlayed those skills into a living for yourself and possibly others. Like a business of any size if you are to succeed in the future, then replenishing, enhancing and marketing that inventory of skills will be required.

If you choose to view yourself as independent, a *company of one*, your choice may require an uncomfortable shift in thinking concerning your relationship with your organization, a shift from employee/employer to independent contractor/client. This shift to being independent, being a *company of one*, requires you to take responsibility for your work life. In return for taking responsibility, you obtain control — one of life's great bargains.

You will want to read this book as an active participant, rather than as a passive bystander. Challenge yourself to become even more independent.

The more we depend on an external organization to make us secure, happy, fulfilled, productive and satisfied, the less need or desire we will have to care for ourselves. If we are not caring for ourselves, who is?

For mutual benefit, work to help your current

employer move from the employer/employee relationship to the independent contractor/client relationship. Become excited and passionate enough to do something about being your own business. Formalize and officially choose what has been true all along — you are independent, a COMPANY OF ONE.

INDEPENDENCE: WHAT IT IS AND WHAT IT ISN'T

The American Heritage dictionary defines independent as, "Free from influence, guidance, or control of another or others; self reliant."

The "another or others" in the context of this book is the salary paying organization.

Being independent is NOT meant to be defined in terms of gender, geography, race, culture, family, psychology, learning style, philosophy, politics, age, religion, social style, etc.

Independent, as used in this book, simply means *to what degree do we, the workers, perceive ourselves to be free from the "influence, guidance, or control" of the organization that pays our salary.* How self-reliant are we judged by where we see the source of our financial security? Do we each see ourselves as *a company of one*?

Are we working for our organizations because we *want* to or because we *have* to?

That's what independence is and that's what it isn't.

IT IS TIME FOR INDEPENDENCE

O. K., so we've tried:

- Taylor's Scientific Management
- Quantitative Management
- Theory X/Y/Z • Managerial Grid
- Quality Circles • Open Door Policies
- Excellence — anything and everything
- Self-Directed/Managed Work Teams
- Total Quality Management (TQM)
- Self-Renewing and Reinventing the Corporation
- Downsizing/Rightsizing/Resizing/Restructuring/ Centralizing/Decentralizing the Organization
- Management by Objectives (MBO)
- Matrix Management
- Japanese Management

- Management by Wandering Around (MBWA)
- The Heroic Manager
- The One Minute Manager
- The Androgenous Manager
- Situational Leadership
- Authoritarian/Participative/Transformational/ Breakthrough Leadership with a topping of Attila the Hun/Abe Lincoln Leadership Principles.

So, how's it going?

Given all the time, energy and expense devoted to increasing professional productivity and personal quality of life, are workers today:

- More dedicated to organizational objectives than a decade ago?

- Willing to give more of their discretionary effort to the job?

- More energized, passionate and focused?

- More willing to risk and to engage in open, honest communications?

- Embracing the growth benefits of change?

- Accepting failure as necessary for learning?

- Feeling better about themselves?

- Less insecure, frustrated, confused, angry and stressed?

From my experience dealing with thousands of workers in both public and private sectors, I believe the majority of today's workers would say "no." While we are making progress, and what we read tells us the new workers are highly educated therefore more mobile and independent, the progress is slow at best.

If we keep doing what we're doing, we'll keep getting what we got. If we continue to apply external concepts to ourselves and others and if we continue to let others dictate to us about what will work for us, we will continue to "get what we got."

If what we got is working, carry on. If not...

It's time to do something else!

- It's time to stop blindly accepting the concept du jour, hoping for the organizationally imposed quick fix. Quick fixes equal temporary results. We have played the external game in isolation long enough.

- It's time we concentrate our energy on becoming internally committed to accomplishing organizational and personal goals because we *want* to rather than perceiving we *have* to.

• It's time we stopped blaming the organization for its suppressive systems and controlling environment and acknowledge the fact that **the systems and the environment are the cumulative creation of each and every individual who together makes up the organization.**

• It's time we as individuals looked to ourselves for the motivation and skills that will improve our quality of life as well as increase our organizational productivity.

• It's time we changed employee/organization relationships from dependent to independent.

• It's time we took control.

• It's time we each became a *company of one*.

THE INDEPENDENCE PARADOX

"Most of Our People Do Not."

The workshop I was facilitating for senior, middle-level managers of a corporation large enough to know better was running along smoothly until quite by accident the discussion evolved into the subject of employee independence. My gut reaction was we needed more workers independent of their organizations if the organizations were to remain effective in the years to come.

The managers said such thinking was fine for me

because I had talent enough to succeed outside of corporate life, if my independence created that situation. Then they added, "Most of our people do not."

At the time my thinking was not as clear on the subject as it is now. I greeted that statement merely as curious and let it go. But the concept that these managers did not believe their people were talented enough to carve out a life outside of their current organization began to nibble away at that portion of my brain that houses curious statements.

What did that belief say about the organization, about the managers, and about the employees?

To me their belief said they have:

- An organization hard-up enough to employ people who are otherwise unemployable.

- Managers who obviously do not view their roles as developing people to expand beyond their jobs. (If these managers had tried, they were not very good at developing employability.)

- A work force that is so unsure of itself, it puts its future in the hands of executive strangers.

Viewed in that light, my thinking accelerated from curious to critical.

Creating independent employees (i.e. employees independent of their organizations) may well need to be the main focus of North American employers in the years to come, if business as we know it is to survive.

We are not talking about employees becoming independent so they *will* leave their jobs. We are talking about employees becoming independent so they *can* leave — critical difference. They would stay because they *want* to, not because they *have* to.

CREATING INDEPENDENT EMPLOYEES MAY WELL NEED TO BE THE MAIN FOCUS OF NORTH AMERICAN EMPLOYERS IN THE YEARS TO COME, IF BUSINESS AS WE KNOW IT IS TO SURVIVE.

How Did We Get Dependent?

Organizations over the years have fostered dependency on the part of employees. This dependency has been created through the use of "control devices." In the late 1800s, business began subsidizing home ownership and corporate workers began "owing their souls to the company store" while government workers settled in for the duration.

I recall when I started in sales the prevailing philosophy was "get a young salesman with a pregnant wife (We were not politically correct in those days.) and a big mortgage because he will work hard and won't leave." Today the "carrots" awarded to those who please the powers-to-be are arguably more sophisticated, i.e. favorable salary classifications, promotions, large offices, executive dining rooms and reserved parking spots.

For years if we performed according to rules of the organization, we could, at the least, maintain our jobs with their economic and emotional benefits for us and our families. At most, we could rise up the corporate ladder increasing our income and prestige thus allowing us to finish our lives with more toys than our neighbors.

The dependency relationship worked because it was mutually beneficial for both the worker and the organization. And if the decision were up to both parties, dependency would probably continue. Dependency is like an old shoe, familiar and comfortable. But like an old shoe, dependency is not always appropriate for all occasions.

The dependency illusion must be eliminated. Who will do the eliminating? The organization can through the elimination of dependency generating policies and procedures. The employee can through the elimination of a false sense of believing security lies within the organization.

WE AS WORKERS ACCEPTED THE CONDITION OF DEPENDENCY AND WE MUST NOW ELIMINATE IT.

The Independence Paradox

The organizations of today are faced with the independence paradox. THEY NEED INDEPENDENT PEOPLE WHO ARE DEPENDENT. Organizations need the innovative, creative, risk-taking sense of ownership independence generates yet want the subordination, faith and blind trust dependence fosters.

Obviously by the definitions of dependence and independence, having both at the same time is impossible; and organizations are finding increasing difficulty getting either.

Getting full commitment to either dependence or independence is difficult because many of today's workers are in passage from dependence to independence.

People realize, some later than others, that they cannot depend on their organizations for financial and emotional security. They also have not as yet accepted the true source of their independence — themselves. For the good of the individual and the organization, we need to move through passage as quickly as possible.

THE INDEPENDENCE PARADOX: ORGANIZATIONS TODAY NEED INDEPENDENT PEOPLE WHO ARE DEPENDENT.

Isn't Independence Tough on Organizations?

At first thought, highly independent employees may seem like characters in a Steven King novel who appear to have risen from the dead to eat the heart out of the organization. I believe the opposite is true. Self-sufficient, independent people are essential to maximize the potential of the organization.

Imagine an entire work force of independent people willing to take risks, to be innovative and creative. Imagine employees so overflowing with open and honest communications they will address those undercurrents of dissatisfaction in the organization that nobody talks about but everybody knows (the organizational "Big Lie").

Will independent employees hinder the organization? No. Independent employees are just what we need in these dynamic, unsettled, restarting times.

INDEPENDENT PEOPLE ARE ESSENTIAL TO MAXIMIZE THE POTENTIAL OF THE ORGANIZATION.

Shouldn't We Strive for Interdependence?

Independent employees, working their way from self-imposed, albeit organizationally fostered, *dependence* on the organization through *independence* of the organization to the ultimate, a partnership or *interdependence* with the organization, are the ideal.

Interdependence equals complete partnership. With interdependence comes unconditional trust and totally open, honest communications along with full confidence in and a genuine respect for the other. (Such a complete partnership as interdependence requires is almost impossible to have if one of the partners is dependent and feels he *has* to be in the partnership.)

According to the prolific writer, Anon., there are no unrealistic goals only unrealistic time frames. The goal of interdependence between employee and organization is realistic. To think it will happen in our work life is unrealistic considering all the baggage most of us carry around on our jobs. We will have to be history before our organizations will be truly forming interdependent employee/employer relationships complete with the necessary doses of trust, communications, confidence and respect.

Again, remembering interdependence is the goal is important. We must continually strive for interdependence but the trip from dependence to interdependence requires a stop at independence. We must feel the self-confidence generated by personal independence before we can participate fully in true interdependence.

The purpose of our time together is to provide the motivation and the knowledge to move us, as today's workers regardless of our places in organizations, along the continuum from dependence to a greater degree of independence. Because experiencing true interdependence with our organizations in the near future is rather impractical, we will leave an indepth discussion of interdependence for another time.

WHILE INTERDEPENDENCE IS THE IDEAL, FOR THE PRESENT, STRIVING FOR INDEPENDENCE IS MOST PRACTICAL.

RECAP

INDEPENDENCE PARADOX

CREATING INDEPENDENT EMPLOYEES MAY WELL NEED TO BE THE MAIN FOCUS OF NORTH AMERICAN EMPLOYERS IN THE YEARS TO COME, IF BUSINESS AS WE KNOW IT IS TO SURVIVE.

■■■

WE AS WORKERS ACCEPTED THE CONDITION OF DEPENDENCY AND WE MUST NOW ELIMINATE IT.

■■■

THE INDEPENDENCE PARADOX: ORGANIZATIONS TODAY NEED INDEPENDENT PEOPLE WHO ARE DEPENDENT.

■■■

INDEPENDENT PEOPLE ARE ESSENTIAL TO MAXIMIZE THE POTENTIAL OF THE ORGANIZATION.

■■■

WHILE INTERDEPENDENCE IS THE IDEAL, FOR THE PRESENT, STRIVING FOR INDEPENDENCE IS MOST PRACTICAL.

ORGANIZATION
What's in it for all of us?

SECTION TWO

ORGANIZATIONAL BENEFITS OF INDEPENDENCE

The Mobile Work Force

After giving a program for Nameless Corporation, I stayed around to listen to a talk by a vice president serving on an executive committee established to return the company to profitability.

The VP listed seven tenets upon which the company turnaround would be based. The first was — the customer would be paramount. The next five covered numeric indexes of company profitability. I waited anxiously with 150 of the employees for mention of the employees and their part in the new, improved company. It finally came. Item seven stated that to hit the numbers some downsizing would occur, but the people affected would be treated with care and compassion.

So, the only part the employees were going to play was when they were let go, it would be with care and compassion. How do you think the dependent workers felt about that?

My first reaction was one of disbelief but that melted into a smidgen of acceptance and even begrudging admiration. Not for one minute did I believe the plan would bring the company to desired profitability over the long run. But I do believe that VP told it exactly the way it was. Numbers improvement through customer focus and tight expense control! Such was the thinking and the plan of the CEO.

The Board of Directors approved the plan which is now the company's marching orders. Those employees currently with the company have been duly informed of what is expected of them.

If they do not wish to spend a significant portion of their lives on earth helping Nameless Corporation gain an X percent rise in productivity or if they can't get excited about helping a legal entity raise its Return on Equity, for the good of all concerned, maybe they should move on.

Ah! There's the rub. DEPENDENT PEOPLE WILL NOT MOVE ON, even though they may violently and with every fiber of their beings despise the emerging culture. They do not believe they have a choice. ("I live in the suburbs, have 2.6 kids, a mini-van, a mortgage and pending college costs. What choice do I have?")

The organization is now relying on an employee to be "empowered," to "do more with less," to "do better faster" when the employee would rather be a shepherd in Wyoming!

The hard question executives are asking is, "How small can our organization be and still get the job done?" The answer to that question will be determined by the commitment of the remaining employees. **The fewer people a downsizing organization has the more committed they have to be.**

Organizations need people on their limited payroll who are there because they want to be not because they have to be, i.e. independent. Organizations need people who can get excited about what obviously excites upper management.

ORGANIZATIONS BENEFIT BECAUSE INDEPENDENT PEOPLE WHO ARE NOT COMMITTED TO THE ORGANIZATION'S MISSION FEEL ABLE TO LEAVE AND NOT REMAIN TO DRAIN LIMITED RESOURCES.

Maslow Revisited

Travel back in time to a classroom. The instructor draws a triangle on the board and gives us our first glimpse of MASLOW'S HIERARCHY OF NEEDS. He draws four horizontal lines inside the triangle thus dividing the triangle into five levels of needs and wants. He then labels the levels.

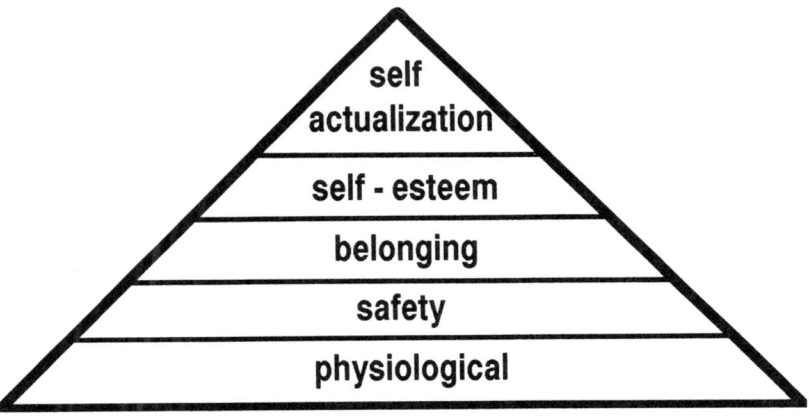

Self-Actualization: Being all we can be.

Self-Esteem: Thinking of ourselves as deserving of recognition and attention, as having value.

Belonging: The desire to love and be loved by somebody.

Safety: The need for physical and emotional well-being.

Physiological: The innate, instinctive needs for food, shelter and warmth.

Abraham Maslow, an author, scholar and past president of the American Psychological Association, contended that all human needs fall into one of these five levels.

So what do Maslow's findings have to do with the benefit of independent employees to organizations?

At what levels of Mazlow's hierarchy are employees most independent of the organization? Are they independent while in the Physiological needs area? How about when they are operating in Safety? Not until employees hit Belonging, Self-Esteem and Self-Actualization can they begin their independence from the organization for which they work.

That's fine for the employee, but of what benefit are "top-of-the-triangle" people to the organization? No benefit — unless the organization wants to get and keep customers.

Every employee in an organization has external and/or internal customers. If he does not have a customer (i.e. somebody whose needs he serves), an excess body is on the payroll.

Organizational Benefits of Independence

For maximum organizational effectiveness at what level of Mazlow's hierarchy and at what level of independence, would employers want employees who are dealing with customers?

When effectively relating to another human being, we need to be more "them" centered than "us" centered. This outward focus, this independence, has a greater chance of occurring the higher up the triangle one goes. How concerned about the needs of another will a person be if he has just been evicted from his house and before nightfall needs to find a refrigerator box for four and a scenic spot under the overpass?

As people move up the triangle, they can take part in problem solving and creativity. Therefore an organization would be most effective in dealing with customers if the employees were operating at least at the Belonging or Self-Esteem (independent) level. (Mazlow contends only two percent of people are Self-Actualized, so let's not kid ourselves.)

Employees should be enjoying the independence that comes with being at either Belonging or Self-Esteem to be most effective and most productive.

What are organizations doing to insure their people have progressed beyond Safety and Physiological needs to Belonging or Self-Esteem?

They are dehiring, downsizing, rightsizing, skill-mix adjusting, redundancy eliminating, work-load imbalance correcting, outsourcing and destaffing.

Organizations are asking employees who remain to swim in unfamiliar waters by "doing more with less," doing "faster, better," doing their jobs as a part of synergistic teams while being innovative, creative and willing to take risks! This is not easy on a dependent person.

One of Maslow's conclusions was: the closer to the bottom the more power the need exerts over behaviors. Having an outwardly focused, confident organization is hard when both hands of the employees are covering their butts, and their heads are turned 180 degrees watching who is gaining on them.

To paraphrase a saying, **"There are only two lasting bequests an organization can hope to give its employees. One of these is roots; the other is wings."** Organizations must give the roots of a stable environment and the wings of independence.

ORGANIZATIONS BENEFIT BECAUSE INDEPENDENT PEOPLE ARE MORE ABLE TO FOCUS ON SATISFYING THE NEEDS OF OTHERS RATHER THAN ON WORRYING ABOUT SAVING THEMSELVES.

Doing Less with More

A manager with four direct reports can expect to exert significant control. (Experts say a manager can manage five to eight dependent people. They are still counting the number of independent people one manager can manage.) Each of the four people, if history is any teacher, can expect to be controlled and to slip easily into a dependent role, dependent on the boss to make any decision of consequence.

Along comes the challenge of downsizing and its resultant need for empowered employees. The manager now has fifteen direct reports. Logistically the manager can not exert the same degree of control. It's now rationally impossible for the employee to expect the same degree of dependence. So while logistically and rationally the employee should not expect control and dependence, emotional acceptance is proving to be another story.

Nancy, a manager who lived that experience, discovered an interesting phenomenon. She found, as had thousands of managers like her, her employees not only did not become more independent when all that was rational dictated they become independent, *they actually became more dependent.*

They "did less with more." They asked more questions, sent more memos, in effect became more immobilized and acted less empowered than ever before. Why would that happen?

Simply, in a downsizing organization in tough economic times, a dependent person is less likely to take risks.

ORGANIZATIONS BENEFIT BECAUSE INDEPENDENT PEOPLE ARE MORE LIKELY TO CHOOSE TO BE EMPOWERED.

Teams of Individuals

While the term "work teams" may soon find itself in buzzword heaven, I believe the "whole being greater than the sum of its parts" is the way of the future.

If teams are to succeed, team members must trust each other; engage in open and honest communications and accept the diversity of others. Team members also need to be creative, innovative, willing to take risks and engage in consensus problem solving/decision making while at the same time proactively seeking new worlds to conquer. Does this sound like the job description for a person attached by an umbilical cord to the organization?

Dependent workers feel they must successfully compete with other team members while conforming with established organizational procedures, or they will be overlooked for raises or promotions. (Even worse, they may be looked at too closely during times of downsizing.)

Dependent workers will soon see the futility of competing with independent workers who perceive they have little to lose.

To build a strong self-sufficient team, the members must push against the limits and possibly even sweep aside policies and procedures created by their own bosses.

The most productive teams are not made up of "yes" people. Independence and approval seeking do not work well together.

ORGANIZATIONS BENEFIT BECAUSE INDEPENDENT PEOPLE ARE MORE EFFECTIVE TEAM MEMBERS.

The Silent Majority

Employees who would speak only under the condition they not be identified...

An unsigned memo was circulated criticizing...

The above phrases were printed in a newspaper article which described some "unrest" at a major U.S. corporation. What is demonstrated in this article are employees legitimately troubled about activities being performed within their company. As loyal and concerned employees, why would they not express their feelings about company policies and procedures? Why did they feel the requirement of anonymity offered by the newspaper? How many unsigned memos and undisclosed sources are alive in your organization?

• Do you believe your coworkers have projects or ideas they are sure would benefit the organization?

• Are some of these potentially beneficial projects or ideas not being implemented or expressed due to concern over what is perceived as a threat to job security?

If the answers to the above questions are "yes," employees believe they have ideas or projects to benefit the organization. But they are so dependent on the approval of the organization for their security they may not feel safe suggesting or implementing potentially beneficial ideas or projects.

If employees are not holding back their potential, both the individuals and, by logical extension, the organization win. If they are holding back out of fear, everyone loses.

Independent workers tend to be more proactive than their dependent brothers and sisters. They do not feel a need for the executive floor to make a decision before acting. This independence increases employee risk-taking, innovation, creativity, problem solving and long-term planning (Some times displaying this empowerment may even mean the elimination of their own jobs.).

When a majority of workers develop an independent mind set, we will witness a significant increase in organizational productivity and a great shift in motivational patterns.

ORGANIZATIONS BENEFIT BECAUSE INDEPENDENT PEOPLE WILLINGLY AND OPENLY COMMUNICATE THEIR IDEAS.

A New Loyalty

When discussing independence in the workplace, the question of loyalty needs to be addressed. Are independent people less loyal to the organization?

No, but they are loyal in a different way. In the past, loyalty has been viewed as: showing up reasonably on time; performing at least the minimum effort to avoid being punished or fired; and not cheating, stealing or "dipping the company pen in the company ink." In turn the organization would be loyal by guaranteeing lifetime employment complete with acceptable salary and benefits.

Organizations began redefining their understanding of loyalty, when because of external conditions, they felt required to repeal lifetime employment and fiddle with workers salaries and benefits. The first employees to go were those who did not live up to the employee side of the loyalty equation, i.e. low performers, morally or legally corrupt. After that, if more cuts were needed, the luck of the draw was a factor. If your position were eliminated, regardless of years of service, exceptional performance and loyalty — you're gone. Your emotional ties to an organization mean nothing when competing against your organization's business interests. For those who stayed, salaries and benefits were either frozen or reduced. So a new loyalty emerged and a new standard of loyalty must be established.

An independent worker is no longer loyal, in the old sense, to a legal entity because the legal entity is not loyal, in the old sense, to him.

In the new world an independent worker must be loyal to a project, a project that will both help develop his skills and aid the organization in the accomplishment of its objectives and its stated mission. An independent worker must be loyal to his values, his code of ethics and morality, and loyal to himself while applying his unique skills to the best of his ability. He must also be loyal to his coworkers by encouraging them to utilize their unique skills.

The organization is loyal to its bottom line.

Is this new brand of loyalty right? No more right or wrong than the perceived old loyalty — it's just different and more powerful. The independent worker, by maximizing her loyalty to her project, herself and her coworkers, will be of greater benefit to the organization than the dependent worker who performed for primarily selfish reasons.

The organization, by focusing on its bottom line,

will be able to provide an economically stable environment in which the independent employee can flourish as long as there is mutual benefit. Since this symbiotic relationship is closer to current reality and, if we are brutally honest, closer to the way employee/employer relationships have been all along, accepting this new independent relationship, this new loyalty, should not be difficult.

ORGANIZATIONS BENEFIT BECAUSE INDEPENDENT PEOPLE ARE LOYAL TO MUTUALLY BENEFICIAL RESULTS, NOT TO A LEGAL ENTITY.

Compensate Our Way to Productivity

How many people do you know who work for an organization that compensates them with a straight salary?

(While recognizing many non-economic compensations are available, for the purpose of this chapter, let's stick to cold, hard cash.)

Studies have proven the payment of a straight salary has the lowest motivational value of any of the standard compensation packages. While this finding is not a surprise to anyone who has worked under other pay systems, the surprise is eighty percent of United States organizations compensate most workers with straight salaries.

Could it be most workers do not have enough independence, enough self-confidence and enough belief in their personal or team's potential to push for a pay-for-performance plan?

Could it mean most organizations want to keep the work force dependent on a steady stream of income or do not have enough confidence in their own workers to implement a pay-for-performance plan?

A *company of one* knows she has to perform to be compensated for her efforts. The better she meets the needs of her "customer" (her organization), the more "business" (money) she will receive.

If you were running a business and the customers were going to pay you for minimum effort, how interested would you be in putting out more than the minimum effort? **If you were a tightrope walker, would you be more interested in performing every move to the best of your ability if you had a safety net? Would you try harder if you didn't have one?**

Straight salary is a poorly used motivational tool whether applied to individuals or teams, but one most desired by dependent employees and most provided by dependent work cultures.

Independent self-confident people making up an independent work culture will push for pay-for-performance compensation to insure maximum effort to the benefit of all involved.

ORGANIZATIONS BENEFIT BECAUSE INDEPENDENT PEOPLE ARE MORE MOTIVATED CONSISTENTLY TO PERFORM AT THEIR BEST. MAXIMIZING PERFORMANCE MAXIMIZES RESULTS.

RECAP

ORGANIZATIONS BENEFIT:

● BECAUSE INDEPENDENT PEOPLE WHO ARE NOT COMMITTED TO THE ORGANIZATION'S MISSION FEEL ABLE TO LEAVE AND NOT REMAIN TO DRAIN LIMITED RESOURCES.

● BECAUSE INDEPENDENT PEOPLE ARE MORE ABLE TO FOCUS ON SATISFYING THE NEEDS OF OTHERS RATHER THAN ON WORRYING ABOUT SAVING THEMSELVES.

● BECAUSE INDEPENDENT PEOPLE ARE MORE LIKELY TO CHOOSE TO BE EMPOWERED.

● BECAUSE INDEPENDENT PEOPLE ARE MORE EFFECTIVE TEAM MEMBERS.

● BECAUSE INDEPENDENT PEOPLE WILLING-

LY AND OPENLY COMMUNICATE THEIR IDEAS.

● BECAUSE INDEPENDENT PEOPLE ARE LOYAL TO MUTUALLY BENEFICIAL RESULTS, NOT TO A LEGAL ENTITY.

● BECAUSE INDEPENDENT PEOPLE ARE MORE MOTIVATED CONSISTENTLY TO PERFORM AT THEIR BEST. MAXIMIZING PERFORMANCE MAXIMIZES RESULTS.

6

ORGANIZATIONAL DOWNSIDES OF A CULTURE OF INDEPENDENCE

If the benefits to an organization for having an independent culture are so great, why would any organization mire itself in the muck of dependence?

Simply answered — it's easier, the "bird in the hand" syndrome. We know what we have. The benefits of dependence, while rapidly dwindling, are certain. The benefits of independence, while essential, may be perceived as a gamble.

Two prerequisites for organizational cultural change, neither of which is considered to be in abundance in many of today's organizations, are time and money.

Time — An ingrained culture which contains a pattern of motivating through fear of loss of security must be changed. Culture change takes time.

The fact many organizations motivate their work force through the fear of losing security would be denied by most of the inhabitants of the large offices but that doesn't make it any less a fact. Motivation through fear is not overt in most cases and not the fault of the organizations.

Organizations have over the years filled the role of benevolent dictators, and the workers have allowed that role to occur. The motivation, "Do what we say or you will lose something," evolved because it worked.

Evolution will be the game plan for moving to independence and to evolve takes time. If taking valuable time is not enough of a deterrent, while the clock is running there may be:

- Increases in mistakes due to added innovation, creativity and risk taking.

- Longer initial project time frames due to workers testing and questioning policies and procedures.

- A temporary reduction in productivity until new work relationships, norms and skills are established.

<u>Money</u> — Budgets may need to be developed, increased or redirected to:

- Cover the new skills required of independent workers and their management.

- Cover the cost of hiring and training new workers, due to a potential increase in turnover.

- Initially develop and implement a new reward structure to hold on to workers who are staying because they want to not because they have to.

While the downsides to a culture of independence, time and money, are formidable, addressing these issues is essential. **To survive and flourish in the world of tomorrow, the question is not *if* an organization adopts a culture of independence, the question is *when*.**

7

HOW TO CREATE AN ORGANIZATIONAL CULTURE OF INDEPENDENCE

■ Create a norm of independence from the top down. Encourage and reward people for challenging policies, testing limits and redrawing organizational parameters. Allocate budgets for funding the development, incubation and implementation of innovative, creative ideas.

■ Reduce health care and pension plans. Provide information and direction on how employees can care for themselves in these areas, e.g. cafeteria plans. Institute flexible, movable retirement plans.

■ Develop a shared and committed to organizational vision with each employee so the employee is not dependent on the leader's dream for meaning and substance. When the employee is committed to a vision she believes has meaning and the leader leaves (a distinct possibility in these times), the employee still has a sense of direction and passion and can operate independently.

■ Eliminate "size-by-title" offices, executive dining rooms, reserved parking spots. These manifestations of relative importance only serve as a reminder of the dependency relationship. The more a person has, the more he perceives he needs.

■ Reduce rules, policies, procedures, reviews, reports, approvals, handbooks, and, yes, management layers. The less rigid, less structured and less layered the organization is, the more the need for employee independence increases.

■ Promote basic and advanced educational opportunities both inside and outside of the work environment and inside and outside job-descripted areas.

(Organizations may fear educating a mobile work force and employees may perceive it a waste of time to educate themselves for jobs that might disappear. Such thinking is both short-sighted and critically flawed.)

- Provide projects with which a worker can personally identify rather than identifying with the organization. Since the individual owns project skills, he can apply these skills both inside and outside of the organization.

- Work with employees at updating résumés and practicing interviewing skills — a good project for the organization's Human Resource professionals.

- Design organizational training to include both skill and growth training. Teach people how to succeed outside of the organization. If they do not stay employed, they should at least be employable.

- Analyze and eliminate, if appropriate, controlling management style. **Controlling managers create dependent employees**.

- Encourage workers to interview for other jobs, both inside and outside of the organization. Move people often within the organization, i.e. build in a lack of externally generated security. Remember independence is the norm.

- Use the goal setting process to aid in creating independence — set high, worthwhile, meaningful, agreed upon and committed to goals. Leave the "how to" to the employee consistent with worker maturity considering legal, moral and organizational values. Monitor the results only.

- Keep employees informed (and train them, if necessary) about the financial status of the organization. Each worker contributes something to the economic well-being of her organization. Knowing how she is doing helps her keep score and such feedback adds input to her decision to commit to organizational goals.

- Encourage telecommuting whenever possible. Physical absence encourages independence of the employee and the organization.

- Re-evaluate the "promote from within" policy. Apologies to Tom Peters, but your best people might not be on your payroll. Your best people may be on somebody else's payroll. On your payroll may be some other organization's best people.

- Create a positive work culture — catch people doing things right. Don't let team members put themselves down. A positive culture which helps individuals feel better about themselves and their abilities is an active ingredient to independence. As the bumper sticker says, "Say *no* to negativity."

PERSONAL
What's in it for me?

SECTION THREE

8

PERSONAL BENEFITS OF INDEPENDENCE

The Monkeys in the Jar

There is a story which may or may not be true but it does make a point, so humor me.

A tribe of African natives would capture monkeys for subsequent sale to a zoo by placing berries in large, heavy jugs with big bottoms and small, top openings. A monkey would reach in and grab a fist full of the berries. Due to the size of the small jug opening and the monkey's comparatively large fist, it couldn't get its furry mitt out of the jug. Not wanting to release the berries and not being able to drag the heavy jug, the monkey would just sit until captured.

The metaphor fans may be well ahead on this one. Just sitting on the ground of the organizational jungle with fists full of benefits and not wishing to release medical and dental "berries" until selected by the natives of the executive floor to go elsewhere is as unfortunate.

We need to "let go," let go of our old way of viewing employee/organization relationships.

INDEPENDENT PEOPLE BENEFIT BECAUSE THEY ARE MORE ABLE TO "LET GO" OF A SITUATION THAT IS NOT BENEFICIAL.

The Control/Stress Relationship

Have you ever spoken to someone who was under negative stress — maybe in the mirror this morning? It's a sure bet that somewhere in that conversation either directly or between the lines came the statement "not in control" or "not in charge." When we're not in control, we tend to experience negative stress, the less control, the more stress.

Control as used here means our ability to make something happen or to stop something from happening when we want it to happen or do not want it to happen — total control. When used in that context, how much control does the average worker have over his or her organization?

If we put ourselves in a position of being dependent on an organization for our security and we have no control over that organization, we therefore have no control over our security — stressful position in which to be.

One of the toughest questions we, as humans, may have to answer in our trek through life is — "What do we control and what don't we control?"

Passing over the metaphysical aspects of that question, the question we are dealing with today is — "Do we control our organizations?" **If we don't control our organizations, is it in our best interest to be dependent upon them?**

The stress caused by being dependent on organizations over which we have no control could create exactly what we don't want to have happen.

dependent = no control
no control = negative stress
negative stress = reduction in performance
reduction in performance = job termination

We can be so dependent on our organizations that we lose our jobs!

Suggestion: choose independence. We still won't have any control over organizations and what they choose to do, but we will have control over how we relate to organizations and their places in our lives. This change in our emotional and mental relationship with organizations will dramatically reduce negative stress and we will get what we want:

independence = control
control = positive stress
positive stress = increase in performance
increase in performance = job stability

We can be so independent of our organizations that we thrive on jobs we want but don't need. Isn't life interesting?

The same process follows for our physical health:

independence = control
control = less negative stress
less negative stress = more relaxed
more relaxed = better health

Healthier and more productive is a combination that leads to a more balanced life. Now we can spend valuable time enjoying the various non-financial elements of our humanity, i.e. emotional, intellectual, social, spiritual and physical instead of desperately trying to hang on to job security we do not control.

I have heard many people employed by organizations express a desire to have their own businesses, but they weren't willing to take the risk. Forming your *company of one,* being your own business, with your current employer as your only client reduces risk while at the same time providing the control of an entrepreneur. A hard-to-beat combination!

INDEPENDENT PEOPLE BENEFIT BECAUSE THEY EXERT MORE CONTROL OVER THEIR LIVES THEREBY EXPERIENCE LESS NEGATIVE STRESS.

Why Choose Independence?

In the good old days when we joined established organizations, we would almost have had to know somebody to get fired. Those days may come again in our business lifetimes but that's not the way to bet. The organization as "lean and mean" in either the public or private sector is the wave of the future for most of us. Why did this happen?

Organizations are downsizing because downsizing is:

1) necessary — Profitability requires a close watch on expenses. Salary is a big chunk of expenses.

2) possible — Advanced technology and competitors cutting back are a reality.

3) desirable — A smaller organization is easier to manage and to keep focused while remaining close to the products/services end user.

These may be the same three reasons why a person may wish to choose the path of independence from the organization:

1) necessary

• Some of the actions associated with independence (choosing to exhibit creativity, innovation, risk taking, open and honest communications) are what our organizations say they want. If organizations really want and reward what they say they want, perhaps independence will be necessary for above average performance appraisals.

• Independence is necessary for our own sanity because it is more in tune with reality by providing us with increased personal control over our future. Projections from the Bureau of Labor Statistics have shown people will change careers three to five times during their work lives. Dependency on organizations we may be forced to change several times generates negative stress.

2) possible

• Dependence on something outside of ourselves is inherent in the human animal. While we are dependent for our emotional and physical survival on someone or something outside of ourselves for a longer period than most other animals, we do have the power of our humanity to choose independence and to recognize its consequences.

• As the mountain climber said, "I climbed the mountain because it was there." Independence along with the control it gives is "there" for the choosing.

3) desirable

• Independence provides an opportunity for personal growth and for increased self-esteem by allowing us actively to seek new challenges, to test personal and organizational limits and to maximize potential. If we choose independence from the organization, this degree of growth is much easier to accomplish.

• Independence creates proactive people who feel a genuine responsibility for the success of the organization. They are choosing to be employed because they want to be. Dependency keeps people reactive, doing what they are told. They are employed because they perceive they need to be. People who choose organizational dependency wait and act on the future of someone else's creation.

INDEPENDENT PEOPLE BENEFIT BECAUSE THEY ARE DOING WHAT IS IN THEIR BEST INTERESTS.

Who Is Going To Do All the Work?

As organizations downsize, where is all the work going? The people leaving certainly did not take the work with them. Here the "phantom limb" syndrome comes into being. Just as the body feels sensations as if a missing limb is still attached, the organization may act as if the old work force is still present and may continue to send work to the downsized group.

Some of this work will remain within the organization and be redistributed to "empowered" full time or part time folks who will be busy "doing more with less." Other work, not essential to the mission of the organization, will be contracted out in its entirety.

How is that working? Look at the relative growth of the core business versus independent contractors. For a variety of reasons the self-employed are currently growing at four times the rate of salaried workers. Where is the work going? The work is going to the companies of one, two, three and four.

Independence is closer to objective reality. Security is not and never has been solely in the hands of the organization. We have always brought certain unique skills to jobs and were paid for those skills. Since the skills were ours, we also had the right and ability to take those skills anywhere we wanted to take them.

INDEPENDENT PEOPLE BENEFIT BECAUSE THEY ARE IN THE BEST POSITION TO CONTINUE DOING WORK THAT IS MEANINGFUL TO THEM.

R-E-S-P-E-C-T

Do organizations respect the old dependable work horses, the employees to whom the organization can do just about anything? Do organizations respect employees who will take anything because they are dependent and perceive they have no place else to go?

Do organizations respect the employee who will:

- Take any assignment without questioning the personal benefit of the new job?

- Accept the promotion of a coworker rather than him as "they must know better"?

- Put up with a reaming because "she's the boss"?

- Fill out every report without having any idea of the reason for the report?

- Acquiesce to any team member's suggestion?

Does the organization respect employees who:

- Are burdened with an almost terminal case of old

loyalty?

- Will not test the limits of organizational policy?
- Will not stand up for the proper application of their unique skills?
- Appear to have a mission of hanging on until they can retire?

For a test to determine if your organization does respect the dependable work horses, look around at who is being promoted.

INDEPENDENT PEOPLE BENEFIT BECAUSE THEY DESERVE AND GET BOTH PERSONAL AND ORGANIZATIONAL RESPECT.

Retraining the Organization

Both employees and the organization have roles to play in the transition from a relationship of dependence to one of independence, but the change must start with the employee.

The employees are the catalysts for this relationship change because the employees are what make up the organization. That obvious fact aside, I happen to believe we as human beings are treated by people as we have taught people to treat us. To carry that axiom further, we are treated by our organizations as we have taught our organizations to treat us. Did we teach we are independent ("I'll take care of me.") or dependent ("You take care of me.")?

Those who are "longer of tooth" were scared during the depression years. They passed on that fear to their children through advice such as — "Get yourself a good secure job with a big company or, better yet, with the government." So we sought lifetime job security with guaranteed cost of living increases and federally guaranteed savings while helping the insurance industry prosper. Dependency became a fixation.

Personal Benefits of Independence

As important as control is for us, we willingly gave it to our organizations because we believed we were buying all important security in return (another interesting life lesson). **Since we do not have the security we desired, shouldn't we get the control back?**

Independence provides more choices thereby reducing the victim role. Life is now not something that happens to us; it becomes an experience of our own making. While we can't blame others, we get control — an excellent trade-off.

Many employees, through this over concern with job security, have trained organizations to rely on employee dependency as a motivational tool. Therefore, if there are to be the creative, innovative, risk-taking and growth-oriented work environments so desired and required in today's changing work environment, each employee must "retrain" her organization by reducing personal dependency on the organization.

How would your organization motivate you if you won the $40 million lottery and your bosses saw you as a significant contributor and wanted you to remain on the payroll?

Common answers to that question state the organization would have to provide a work environment that was challenging, provided learning and was fun.

The organization would also have to provide a work environment in which a person would want to work (independent) rather than a threatening environment in which a person perceives he has to work (dependent).

If employees expect their organizations to work hard at creating challenging, educational and fun environments, employees must win the lottery or commit to retraining their organizations.

INDEPENDENT PEOPLE BENEFIT BECAUSE THEY ARE TREATED BY THEIR ORGANIZATIONS AS THEY WISH TO BE TREATED.

A Country Drug Store

When thinking of a *company of one*, the similarities to a small country drug store come to mind. The drug store has a certain inventory to sell:

prescription drugs
snack foods
tobacco
liquor
toiletries
etc.

When analyzing their business, the owners of the drug store determine that prescription drugs and toiletries accounted for over seventy-five percent of their profit.

Enter a large chain discount store. With the buying volume of the large store, they are able to undercut severely the small store's prescription and toiletries prices. The customers, being loyal to their pocketbooks, follow the low prices. What is the small store to do?

They can't cut prices any more. Either they find customers who don't care about price, go out of business or... or they begin to rely on their uniqueness and their other inventory items perhaps choosing to add to their inventory to keep them in business.

How does this apply to a *company of one?* Mike Campbell is in business as systems analyst for state government. Mike's *company of one* (named Mikey Likes It) has certain inventory to sell:

technical knowledge
problem-solving ability
creativity
communications skills
speed reading
carpentry
computer expertise
etc.

When analyzing his *company of one*, Mike determined that technical knowledge, problem solving and computer expertise utilized in his position of systems analyst accounted for 100 percent of his income. Enter a slower economy with voter-induced downsizing and systems analyst work is being contracted out. What is Mike to do?

His *company of one* lost its only client. Either he finds another client who is not affected by the economy, negotiates as an independent contractor with his old client, goes out of business or... or Mike begins to rely on his uniqueness and his other inventory items perhaps choosing to expand his inventory to stay in business.

INDEPENDENT PEOPLE BENEFIT BECAUSE THEY RECOGNIZE, CULTIVATE AND USE THEIR OPTIONS.

A Big Mistake

Dependency is carried to an extreme when the organization becomes the source of our identity. If we identify with an organization and not with our own unique skills, leaving that organization for their reasons or ours will be extremely difficult. If we are no longer with the company — "Who are we? What can we do now?"

Thinking we are working for someone else is a big mistake. We all have our own personal hopes and dreams. We use our work to satisfy those hopes and dreams through the financial security and/or the emotional satisfaction the work provides. Regardless of where we derive our salary, we are really working for ourselves.

When we choose independence, we are working at jobs that to us have real meaning or we wouldn't stay. Our self-esteem is increased because we are voluntarily giving of our discretionary effort. We are not selling out for money because life holds more promise.

Work is a means to an end, not the end itself. The end is the substance of our lives; our substance is what we are about, our personal purpose. **Work is a means to that end. We must be free to pursue other means at our discretion if our end is not being met.** Not fulfilling our personal purpose and feeling we are not free to adjust our means, makes us prisoners in our own lives.

INDEPENDENT PEOPLE BENEFIT BECAUSE THEY POSSESS THE ABILITY TO ACT ON THEIR OWN HOPES AND DREAMS, NOT SOMEBODY ELSE'S.

RECAP

INDEPENDENT PEOPLE BENEFIT:

- BECAUSE THEY ARE MORE ABLE TO "LET GO" OF A SITUATION THAT IS NOT BENEFICIAL.

- BECAUSE THEY EXERT MORE CONTROL OVER THEIR LIVES THEREBY EXPERIENCE LESS NEGATIVE STRESS.

- BECAUSE THEY ARE DOING WHAT IS IN THEIR BEST INTERESTS.

- BECAUSE THEY ARE IN THE BEST POSITION TO CONTINUE DOING WORK THAT IS MEANINGFUL TO THEM.

- BECAUSE THEY DESERVE AND GET BOTH PERSONAL AND ORGANIZATIONAL RESPECT.

- **BECAUSE THEY ARE TREATED BY THEIR ORGANIZATIONS AS THEY WISH TO BE TREATED.**

- **BECAUSE THEY RECOGNIZE, CULTIVATE AND USE THEIR OPTIONS.**

- **BECAUSE THEY POSSESS THE ABILITY TO ACT ON THEIR OWN HOPES AND DREAMS, NOT SOMEBODY ELSE'S.**

9

PERSONAL DOWNSIDES OF INDEPENDENCE

If independence is so good, why are so many people still dependent?

■ Independence eliminates excuses. When a person is independent, thus without others to blame, there are no excuses for:

- stress-induced negative behaviors (drinking, drugs, hostility, withdrawal, etc.).

- stress-induced illnesses (hypertension, heart attacks, colitis, ulcers, etc.).

- immobilization on the job.

- complaining about everything and everybody.

- workaholism.

No excuses, period.

■ Independent people have to take time in the present to plan for the future. Where are we now? Where do we want to be and what will it take to get us there? This planning involves self-analysis, a highly beneficial but often ignored process due to time and the potential agony of introspection.

■ Being independent may be harmful to our health.

- We may have to go through the gut-wrenching ordeal of changing self-image. If we have been dependent all of our work lives, see ourselves as dependent and choose independence, over the short run, internal harmony is disrupted.

- If we choose independence and our self-image is consistent with that choice but our organization has chosen a culture of dependence, we are put in an unenviable position of working all day supporting an organizational culture we would like to change. To choose independence and choose to continue to work in a dependent culture requiring dependent behaviors is a perfect set-up for personal and professional burnout. This dissidence causes disharmony. There exists a difference between what we are choosing to believe internally and what we are choosing to do externally.

In my opinion, **the lack of harmony between the internal belief and the external behavior is one of the major causes of negative stress and its resultant reduced level of productivity in work life today.**

- Independent people may experience change in relationships with dependent coworkers. Work values will be different.

- Independent people must always be ready to leave. Knowing that we can relocate when there ceases to be mutual benefits puts certain pressures on us to be proactive by constantly analyzing our current situations to determine if the mutual benefits still exists.

Independence will require extra effort to keep our inventories of skills updated, saleable and of high quality. Since our current organizations may be our only clients and those relationships, as with any independent contractor/client relationships, could end at any time, we must also be responsible for choosing other potential clients to whom to market our inventories. We know what skills we need to survive on our current jobs. What else do we need to know to be saleable elsewhere? When we make that determination, we need to obtain those skills. This new found feeling of mobility, skill updating,

Personal Downsides of Independence

client prospecting and recommitting to the organization daily can be tiring.

- Independent people may have this irresistible urge to work harder. Remember working for an organization is now our idea. We're working because we want to. The "our choice" mind-set tends to inspire us to greater efforts because we are excited about what we do, otherwise we wouldn't do it.

- Independent people may need to invest money and time into enhancing and/or adding to their inventories of skills. Also they may need to create or designate a portion of the personal budget as a "go to hell" fund and keep the balance high enough to achieve an acceptable level of personal financial security.

- Independent people need to develop new friends and acquaintances with whom to network. We tend to surround ourselves with people who are like us. If we are dependent, the bulk of our friends and acquaintances may be the same.

Are the upsides worth the downsides? If so, move on to the next chapter. If not, commit to a work life of dependency.

10

HOW TO CREATE A PERSONAL CULTURE OF INDEPENDENCE

■ Take advantage of all educational opportunities both inside and outside of the organization. The days of the organization providing all the training needs of an employee are gone the way of guaranteed employment. Being independent does not negatively affect those with marketable skills.

■ Develop a clear understanding of personal purpose. We all have a personal purpose which understood or not is already operational. Does our personal purpose allow us to see ourselves as independent? When we wallow in the dependence dumpster, seeing ourselves any other way is difficult. Larger organizations must have a purpose, should not a *company of one*? Along with the purpose, create the other four functions of an organization, i.e. goals, feedback, rewards and support.

■ Have fun with your *company of one*. Give it a name; have business cards printed; keep financial records. Treat yourself as you truly are, a combination of marketable skills.

■ What do you have going for yourself? Take time for self-analysis. Because of the human condition, being abnormal is being normal. What are your unique skills? After you have developed your list, ask people who know you well to comment on and add to the list. Then begin to demonstrate your skills not just within your work group, but also outside.

■ See your job as upper management might see your job. See your job as a *company of one*. Research:

- What organizational (client) problems your *company of one* solves.

- How your *company of one* currently contributes to the accomplishment of the organizational (client) objectives and how it can contribute in the future.

- How the organization (client) would suffer if your

company of one did not exist.

Discuss this information with your boss.

■ Prepare or update your résumé. Considering the volatility in the job market there should not be one employed person without an updated résumé or its equivalent. People should be marketing their *company of one* by reading want-ads and interviewing both inside and outside their organizations. They should be networking, joining professional associations, talking to headhunters and looking around their current organizations for jobs not being done which they can offer to do on a contractual basis if that becomes necessary.

■ Put the money issue in its proper perspective by listing all of your current financial assets and liabilities. Then develop a plan individually or with a financial consultant. Plan how you could manage, given your current financial condition, if no money came in as a result of a change in your work relationships for six, twelve, or twenty-four months.

■ Open your consciousness to personal acts of independence. When we look for something, we see much more of it than when we close ourselves off. Be open to the concept of abundance versus scarcity. Be open to the many people you know, have read about, have heard about from friends or on the radio, or have seen on TV who have not only survived leaving one job but have actually flourished. The world is full of people who have hurt for a while but are now fine and wouldn't go back to the old way. Seek out their stories. Keep aware that the best mentors around may be in your own backyard.

■ Plan your career as pool players plan their next shots. Ask about every assignment, "Will this help me on my next job?" This approach may sound selfish, but when are you likely to give your best to an assignment, when it benefits you or the company more? Being "rèsumè aware" when accepting job assignments is mutually beneficial.

■ Volunteer to help others and for every special assignment you can fit in your busy schedule. Accept all growth opportunities. A person learns from everything she does. Keep adding skills to the inventory you have to offer.

■ Broaden your list of friends and business acquaintances so they can stimulate new ideas, new directions and new possibilities. We have all heard of people who attained significant success because they knew somebody. Whom do you know? **Maintain visibility, marketability and mobility.**

■ Truthfully, what would those people who are currently deriving some or all of their financial support from you do if that support disappeared?

Work with them to develop a plan. **It is as tough in its own way to depend as it is to be depended upon.**

Here is an exercise to demonstrate this important point. I included this experience in my book, *From the Inside Out: How to Create and Survive a Culture of Change,* and it is equally appropriate in this setting. Ask someone to stand with feet shoulder width apart, bent over at the waist and "walk out" with his hands until he is evenly supported by both hands and feet. Then ask someone else of about the same height and weight to stand perpendicular to the person doing the imitation of the "Golden Arches" and gently allow his body to lean over the bent back. The person in the down position is like a horse packing a dead soldier.

Then ask the question, "For whom do you feel this position is most uncomfortable?" During the discussion it will become obvious that the positions are uncomfortable for both parties. The one on the bottom feels an obligation to keep the one on the top "secure." The one on the top does not have any control and if he wants to be "secure," the person on the bottom has to be kept contented. The metaphor of the organization feeling a responsibility to keep its employees "up" and the employees' dependence is clear.

Next ask the two volunteers to stand back to back with their shoulders touching slightly and gently lean into the other and feel the support. While the support each participant receives is evident, there is an understanding that each is not dependent on the other for security. If one person were to leave (either the employee or the organization), the form of the relationship would change, but the other would not be devastated.

■ Make a personal Declaration of Independence. Choose independence from your organization over dependence on your organization — this can be done immediately. "I (name) as of (date) choose independence. I will from this day forth plan and execute as a *company of one*."

All the preceding "how to's" will be useless without this choice.

ACTION
Now what do I do?

SECTION FOUR

PERSONAL BUSINESS PLAN

The elements of the following business plan may not be formal and official. The plan is not intended to pry thousands of dollars from a venture capitalist. Completing it, if you are currently employed or would like to be, will get you started at looking at your self as the business you really are, *a company of one.*

Personal Business Plan

Company Name — What will you call this composite of unique skills and talents that is you?

Company Mission — Stated in a few dozen words, what is the image of what you want your *company* *of one* to be in the future. This image should provide direction, inspiration, and excitement while generating commitment. **Your mission in line with the mission of your client(s) is as good as it gets.**

Inventory — What skills, talents, abilities and/or strengths does your *company of one* possess that can be sold or bartered?

(Note: This skills' inventory, if you are not used to self-analysis, may not be as easy as it seems. A suggestion: *What Color is Your Parachute* by Richard Nelson Bolles published by Ten Speed Press. Bolles has made a living updating this book yearly and provides an excellent source for information on conducting a personal skill inventory.)

Current Client(s) — To whom are you currently selling or bartering your inventory?

Potential Clients — To whom would you be able or willing (or really love) to sell or barter your inventory?

Competition — Who else does what you do? What can you do that they can't? What can they do that you can't? (Excellent action plan item)

Potential Income — What income, in the current or immediate future, can you expect from the sales of your inventory?

Action Plan for Enhancing Inventory — What will you do, when will you do it and what will it cost to add to and/or update your inventory?

Marketing Plan — What specifically are you doing or going to do to insure your unique inventory is known and desired by current and potential clients? What dollars will you set aside to insure this essential marketing can happen? What problems do you anticipate? How will you overcome them?

12

NEW EMPLOYMENT CONTRACT

A lot of talk has been going around lately about the "new" employment contract. What is the difference between the new and the old? What is an employment contract anyway? Did we ever have one?

Very few of us have or ever will have the occasion to labor under a written employment contract. At best our contracts are verbal, or are they? I would venture to say that most of us have never even verbalized a contract; it was just something that was "understood."

What did we understand our contract to be? Probably something like — "If I do a good day's work and don't lie or cheat, I am guaranteed employment in a safe environment as long as I want it."

I think we can see where that idea has gone awry. We still must put in a good day's work and still not lie or cheat. Our environment must still be safe but the lifetime employment piece seems a bit shaky. What other changes should be made?

The following pages contain a sample generic employment contract for the new employee/employer relationship and a blank form.

Consider using the blank as a prompt in a group meeting to get feelings out in the open regarding what we expect from the organization and what we will be willing to give in return.

Obviously these contracts are not legally binding but as long as we're going to talk about the new employment contract, we might as well know what we're talking about.

SAMPLE EMPLOYMENT CONTRACT

Contract made as of _____ between first party _Name, Title_
          (date)   (first party)
and second party _Name of Organization._
                                (second party)

First and second party agree:

        The first party agrees to:

Adhere to the rules of the workplace (work hours, smoking/non-smoking, carrying ID cards etc.).

Devote reasonable time and energy required to accomplish mutually (first and second party) agreed upon objectives in a moral and ethical manner.

Address issues openly and honestly.

Stay updated on new technologies, policies, procedures etc.

Refuse all job assignments that do not aid in accomplishment of personal and organizational mission.

Test the limits of the organization to facilitate personal and organizational growth.

        The second party agrees to:

Promote employability not employment.

Provide challenging and meaningful projects.

Provide a safe work environment.

Provide access to the organization's vision and financials.

Keep rules and regulations to a minimum.

Reduce, where appropriate, controlling management styles.

Provide mutually acceptable salary treatment consistent with stakeholder interest.

Signatures:

    First Party   _____

    Date   _____

    Second Party   _____

    Date   _____

    Witness: _____

    Date   _____

EMPLOYMENT CONTRACT

Contract made as of _____ between first party _____
  (date)   (first party)

and second party _____ .
                              (second party)

First and second party agree:

        The first party agrees to:

        The second party agrees to:

Signatures:

    First Party   _____

    Date   _____

    Second Party   _____

    Date   _____

    Witness   _____

    Date   _____

WRAP UP
What else is there to say?

SECTION FIVE

13

INDEPENDENCE — HOW IT SOUNDS ON THE JOB

Situation:
Organization announces a restructuring necessitating a twenty-five percent reduction of personnel.

Dependent Employee:
"After all my years of faithful service, it's just not fair to put me through this. I've done everything they asked and now they're going to throw me out on the street. Don't they care what happens to me? This kind of work is all I know. It's just not fair."

Independent Employee:
"Well this is a dirty trick. It's too bad the organization feels it has to downsize but it's their call to

make; I'm just glad I was ready for it. Since there is a twenty-five percent chance I may have to find another job, I'd better put my plan into affect. I'll recontact those companies that showed interest the last time I did a rèsumè blitz. I'll call my contacts in the professional associations I belong to, and I'm glad I saved the name of that headhunter who called awhile ago. I've got a lot to do. I'd better get busy."

■■■

Situation:
As a result of a severe downsizing, the survivors are being asked to do more with less. To accomplish all that needs to be done, the employees have been "empowered."

Dependent Employee:
"Empowered, that's great! They give me a big fat chance to screw up just when the organization is downsizing. Take risks; try new approaches to old problems; test the limits! Are they nuts? The only reason we're empowered is because of the economy. If the company wasn't hurting, it would be business as usual."

Independent Employee:
"Whether they are actually serious about empowerment or not, or for whatever reason it's being implemented, it's fine with me. This empowerment business gives me permission to test some ideas I

have about improving our results and I've always wanted to see just where my limits are."

■■■

Situation:
As a result of the introduction of Total Quality Management (TQM), work teams have been formed.

Dependent Employee:
"I can't believe it. They want me to put my future in the hands of a bunch of other people! The organization has always paid me to make these decisions and I've never let them down. Why should I waste my valuable time listening to others debate issues they don't know anything about — and then they want a consensus! I sure hope this is just another fad. Maybe if I hang in long enough, teams will be history and the boss will be back relying on me again."

Independent Employee:
"What a good deal this is! I can enhance my skill inventory and get paid for it. By working with a team I learn facts from team mates and I can evaluate their opinions. I learn how to gain agreement without aggravating anyone, how to obtain commitment to a result for the benefit of the organization and I learn to market and sell my ideas — invaluable knowledge for a *company of one*."

Independence - How It Sounds on the Job

Situation:
New technology is introduced into the workplace.

Dependent Employee:
"They want me to help test out some of the new equipment. What a joke! I see where this whole thing is going. Pretty soon they'll think they don't need me. This new equipment is a mistake because technology will never take the place of people, especially not people like me who have given their hearts and souls to this place."

Independent Employee:
"Pretty interesting stuff! It could really change things around here and maybe in our entire industry. I'd better learn as much about it as possible so my *company of one* skills' inventory will be up to date if I need to find a new client."

■■■

Situation:
Due to dramatic changes the organization seems to have lost its vision. Employees feel there is little or no direction.

Dependent Employee:
"How do they expect me to get my job done when they keep changing the ground rules every fifteen minutes. I want to do what the boss wants done,

but she's not giving me any clarification on what that is. This is really frustrating because this is not the time to screw up."

Independent Employee:
"If upper management is clear on what we're suppossed to be doing, they sure aren't communicating it to us. I guess if anything is going to get accomplished around here, I'll have to do it. It's good that I believe it's better to ask forgiveness than permission. I'll put together a mission statement for our team and run it past the boss. If she either agrees or disagrees, I'll have direction. Maybe we can even push mission up the organization."

TRAITS OF AN INDEPENDENT PERSON

- Recognizes true security to be in the quality of her work.

- Recognizes the choices in everything he does.

- Is loyal to a project, team members and self.

- Is committed to doing her best at what is important to her.

- Constantly seeks self-improvement.

- Has a high sense of self-worth/not reliant on the opinions of others.

- Accurately assesses personal strengths and weaknesses.

- Is self-motivated.

- Works confidently with any level in the organization.

- Willingly takes risks to implement ideas or projects he feels will benefit himself and the organization.

- Is honest and open in all communications.

- Has identity separate from the organization.

- Commits to organizational objectives because she wants to not because she has to.

15

WHAT OTHERS HAVE TO SAY....

The reason Wakan Tanka (Great Spirit) does not make two birds or animals alike is because each is placed here by Wakan Tanka to be an independent individual and to rely on itself.
          Shooter — Teton Sioux

If your happiness depends on what somebody else does...you do have a problem.
          Richard Bach

Life is either a daring adventure or nothing.
          Helen Keller

This is the true joy in life — the being used for a purpose recognized by yourself as a mighty one. I want to be thoroughly used up when I die...Rejoice in life for its own sake.
          George Bernard Shaw

Rabbi Zusya said that on the day of judgement, God would ask him, not why he had not been Moses, but why he had not been Zusya.
          Walter Kaufmann

When people are free to do as they please, they usually imitate each other.
          Eric Hoffer

People have one thing in common, they are all different.
          Robert Zend

Why should we be in such desperate haste to succeed, and in such desperate enterprises? If a man does not keep pace with his companions, perhaps he hears a different drummer.
          Henry David Thoreau

I don't know the key to success, but the key to failure is trying to please everybody.
          Bill Cosby

One of the symptoms of an approaching breakdown is the belief that one's work is terribly important.
          Bertrand Russell

What Others Have To Say...

In order to live free and happily you must sacrifice boredom. It's not an easy sacrifice.
    Richard Bach

But if a man happens to find himself...he has a mansion which he can inhabit with dignity all the days of his life.
    James Michener

Trust in Allah, but tie your camel.
    Arabian Proverb

I have to do it myself and I can't do it alone.
    Larry Wilson

Independence is essential for permanent but fatal to immediate success.
    Samuel Butler

If security no longer comes from being employed, it must come from being employable.
    Rosabeth Moss Kanter

You can't please everyone so you got to please yourself.
    Rick Nelson

Life is what happens while you're making other plans.
    John Lennon

Ships in the harbor are safe, but that is not what ships are made for.
    John Shedd

A Company of One

You can't steal second base and keep one foot on first.
    Anon.

Let there be spaces in your togetherness...
And stand together yet not too near together:
For the pillars of the temple stand apart,
And the oak tree and the cypress grow not
 in each other's shadow.
    Kahlil Gibran

"Come to the edge of the cliff," he said.
    "We're afraid," they said.
"Come to the edge of the cliff," he said.
    "We're afraid," they said.
"Come to the edge of the cliff," he said.
    They came.
    He pushed.
    They flew.
    Guillaume Appollinaire

16

SOME LAST WORDS

Earlier in this book the question was asked, "If we don't control our organizations, is it in our best interest to be dependent upon them?"

If reading this book has made any impact, we can answer the question in unison, "NO!" We also know it is not in the best interest of successful organizations to have us dependent upon them.

Intellectually we know the power of a *company of one* for both ourselves and our organizations. But knowing it is not enough. The power of independence in the workplace will only be experienced when we choose independence emotionally and put it into effect physically. When understanding, choosing and doing come together, our personal and professional worlds will never be the same.

While doing research for this book and asking today's workers what they felt to be the major benefit of being a *company of one*, I received an answer that summed up most of the other answers and confirmed my conviction for the need of independence in the workplace. The answer that gave me the passion to complete this project was — "If I were truly independent, I could stop being scared."

A *company of one* is about not being scared; it is hope; it is control; it is productivity; it is reality and it is achievable — whenever we are ready.....Ready?

17

DECLARATION OF INDEPENDENCE

(Special thanks to the forefathers of the U.S.A. for the format.)

THE DECLARATION OF INDEPENDENCE

When in the course of human events, it becomes necessary for people to dissolve the organizational bonds which have connected them with another, and to assume among the powers of the earth, the separate and equal station to which the laws of nature and of nature's God entitle them, a decent respect to the opinions of mankind requires that they should declare the causes which impel them to the separation.

We hold these truths to be self-evident, that all employees are created equal, that they must be endowed by their management with certain unalienable rights that among these are a balanced life, liberty and the pursuit of happiness, that to secure these rights, organizations are instituted among men, deriving their just powers from the consent of the employees, that whenever any form of management becomes destructive of these ends, it is the right of the employee to alter or to abolish it, and to institute a new organizational culture laying its foundation on such principles and organizing its powers in such form as to them shall seem most likely to effect their productivity and happiness.

Prudence indeed will dictate that cultures long established should not be changed for light and transient causes; and accordingly all experience hath shown, that employees are more disposed to suffer, while evils are sufferable, than to right themselves by abolishing the cultures to which they are accustomed.

But when a long train of abuses and usurpations, pursuing invariably the same object evinces a design to reduce them under a culture of dependence, it is their right, it is their duty to throw off such a culture, and to provide new guards for their future Security. Such has been the patient sufferance of many employees; and such is now the necessity which constrains them to alter their former culture of organizational dependence.

I, THEREFORE, do, in my name, and by authority of my rights as a human being, solemnly publish and declare, That I AM FREE AND INDEPENDENT; and that I am absolved from all unnatural allegiance to a business entity; and that as free and independent, I have full power to, take calculated risks, address business issues as I see them, prepare for a life outside of my current employment and to do all other acts and things which independent people may of right do and for the support of this declaration, with a firm reliance on the protection of our own abilities, we independent people mutually pledge to each other our support, our fortunes and our sacred honor.

A COMPANY OF ONE
IS AVAILABLE AS A LIVE PRESENTATION

If you would like to share what you have read, Tom Payne and his staff are available to present to your organization a thought-provoking presentation based on the concepts of *A Company of One*.

Also available are programs based on his previous book, *From the Inside Out: How to Create and Survive a Culture of Change*, and other presentations dealing with the human aspects of organizational issues.

LODESTAR programs are available in a variety of interactive formats ranging from keynote addresses to full week workshops and are designed to meet the specific needs of corporations, professional associations and the general public.

To get additional information on LODESTAR, speeches, workshops, seminars, publications, audio cassettes and consulting or to order additional copies (Quantity discounts available) of *A Company of One* or *From the Inside Out: How To Create and Survive a Culture of Change*, contact:

★
LODESTAR
A Performance Enhancement Company
1200 Lawrence Court NE
Albuquerque, NM 87123-1905
or call
800-447-9254/505-296-2940
FAX   505-294-6942